GW00750636

THE BARBICAN
SITTING ON
HISTORY

JENNIFER CLARKE

Barbican: The outwork intended to defend the drawbridge in a fortified town or castle (French, Barbacane). Also an opening or loophole in the wall of a fortress, through which guns may be fired.

Brewers' Dictionary of Phrase and Fable. 1870.

© Corporation of London
1990

ISBN 0 85203 030 4

Printing and Stationery Department
PSB4152 9/90 5M — MPP

CONTENTS

i would like to acknowledge, with gratitude, the generous support I received from friends, colleagues and neighbours during the research for this book.

My thanks are also due to:
— David Amies, Manager of the Barbican Estate, for his patience and encouragement.
— My father, D. Waldo Clarke, for keeping a careful eye (and providing most of the research) on William Shakespeare.
— Edward Dudley for all his advice, and for stepping into the role of publisher's reader.
— Paul Nixon (helped by Katy Bell), of the Barbican Centre, who worked so hard on the manuscript.
— Monica Willan, whose memories of the area were invaluable.

For other particular help and advice I would like to thank Mary Rose Clackson; the Staff of the Guildhall Library; Jean Langmead; Gavin Morgan of the Museum of London; Charlotte Mayer, Sculptor, and Mark Williams of the Barbican Library.

John Murray (Publishers) Ltd, for permission to quote John Betjeman's poem *City* from *Collected Poems*.

Peters, Fraser, and Dunlop Group Ltd, for permission to quote from *The World My Wilderness* by Rose Macaulay (Collins Publishers, 1950).

The Guildhall Library, Museum of London and Barbican Centre who provided most of the illustrations for this book.

ACKNOWLEDGMENTS

FOREWORD

*i*t is a privilege to be able to introduce and commend this book, written by Jennifer Clarke to mark the Twenty-First Birthday of the Barbican Estate, and published by the Barbican Residential Committee of the Corporation of London.

The authoress has done a remarkable job; nearly 2000 years are covered in these pages, necessarily briefly, but with sufficient detail to point an interested reader along a line of further research into any of the people and incidents described. The years are steeped in history, and the Barbican produces a rich harvest of events, people, activities, life and death in all its forms, and reminders that there is really nothing new under the sun (was it just over 600 years ago that the Poll Tax was so unpopular?).

Here we have much to savour, with characters both famous and infamous moving through the pages hard on each others' heels, brought to life with a skilful pen. The illustrations give colour and depth to the descriptions and again provide encouragement for research.

Of the Barbican Estate itself, none of those living there has been mentioned. How wise — bring in one name and everyone would seek a mention!

The Barbican Estate has come of age. May it continue to play its part in the history of our City.

Benson Catt, JP, FCA, CC,
Chairman of the Barbican Residential Committee

THE BARBICAN

*t*he Barbican in the City of London covers an area of about forty acres. Ten minutes' walk to the south stands St Paul's Cathedral. Close by, on the west side, are Smithfield Meat Market, St. Bartholomew's Hospital and the ancient church of St. Bartholomew The Great. To the east are Moorgate, Bunhill Fields and Liverpool Street. Old Street, Clerkenwell and Islington lie to the north.

During the Second World War the Barbican was almost totally destroyed and, in the late 1950s, the Corporation of the City of London made the unusual decision to build a residential estate on the site. By 1969 the new estate was officially occupied and today some

The Barbican area — 1981.

4,000 people live there in flats ranging from bed-sitters to penthouses. There are three tower blocks, *Lauderdale, Shakespeare* and *Cromwell*, thirteen low-rise blocks, two mews and *The Postern, Wallside* and *Milton Court*. It is a vast and impressive sight, softened, when one ventures into the interior, by gardens, a man-made lake and a church.

Occupying the same area, and part of the original scheme, are the Barbican Centre, the Guildhall School of Music and Drama, the Museum of London and the City of London School for Girls. *The Barbican* therefore, is visited by large numbers of people who do not actually live there and, as a result, is subjected to far greater public scrutiny and interest than most residential estates. This interest not only focuses on the Barbican today, but also on its past. A past that seems to have vanished.

Appearances are deceptive. Some of the old streets, and almost all the old buildings have gone, but the history of the area still flourishes, casually taken for granted by the people who live and work there.

For hundreds of years the name itself, *Barbican*, has been used to identify the area as a whole. The church of St. Giles Cripplegate, standing in the middle of the estate, was founded over nine hundred years ago, built just outside the old wall which separated the *City* from the *Suburbs*.

Three ancient City wards, *Aldersgate, Cripplegate Within* and *Cripplegate Without* make up the Barbican, and residents elect their Common Councilmen by voting at the annual Wardmote. Those elected become representatives on the Court of Common Council at the Guildhall.

The blocks of flats on the estate are named after men who had connections with the area in the past*. Some are very famous indeed — William Shakespeare, Daniel Defoe, Thomas More; but who were John Trundle, George Seddon and Lancelot Andrewes? And what was here, long ago, before the bombs fell and history was almost swept away?

As with most things, it is best to go back to the beginning.

*See Appendix

THE
ROMAN
CONNECTION

THE ROMAN CONNECTION

*b*arbican, Cripplegate, Aldersgate, London Wall and Moorgate — none of these names would exist today if the Romans had not invaded Britain in AD43 and chosen, as one of their settlements, a site on the north bank of the Thames. They called it Londinium and it stood where the City of London stands today.

During a fierce and bloody war of retribution, the first town and port were destroyed by British tribes, the Iceni, led by Queen Boudicca, and the Trinovantes from Essex. Once the rebellion had been suppressed, Londinium was rebuilt and soon became an important financial centre for the province and then for the whole of Britain.

The Romans then added a military fort

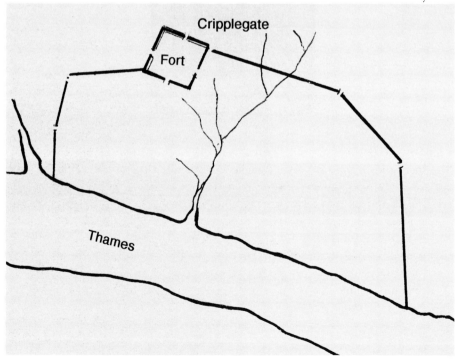

and barracks, situated to the north-west of the town. Rectangular in shape, with rounded corners, it covered about eleven acres, with a tower at each corner and a gate in each side. The northerly gate later became known as Cripplegate. When they also built a high encircling wall, the north and west sides of the fort were included as part of the design.

By the beginning of the fifth century the Roman administration was disintegrating and the Saxon conquest had already begun. The great wall round London remained, but the fort gradually fell into disuse, its south and east sides crumbling, until they vanished and were forgotten. The only evidence that the fort had existed was an unusual right-angle in one particular stretch of the wall — and a gate or *postern*. No one knows who, if anyone, lived in the area later known as the Barbican, which lay just outside this gate. Much of it was moorland, wet and marshy, and not likely to attract many inhabitants.

London itself continued to survive, if at times somewhat grimly. The Saxons established themselves, Christianity arrived and St. Paul's church was founded. Then the Danes invaded and London was attacked and burned. A final Danish conquest in 1017 brought King Canute to the throne, followed by the long reign of Edward the Confessor.

In October 1066 Harold Godwinson, last of the Saxon kings, marched out of London with his army to resist the invasion of William of Normandy. The history of the Barbican was about to begin.

City Roman Wall and defences.

THE
ELEVENTH-FIFTEENTH
CENTURIES

*William the Conqueror in his charter
to the college of St Marten le Grand,
in London, hath these words: "I do
give and grant to the same church
all the land and the moor without
the postern, which is called
Cripplegate . . .*
John Stow: "A Survey of London".
(First published 1598)

*The wall is high and great, well
towered on the north side, with due
distances between the towers.*
William Fitzstephen 1174

THE
ELEVENTH-
FIFTEENTH
CENTURIES

*f*or some time after the Norman Conquest the "land and the moor without the postern" saw little change. Inside the wall, new buildings were going up with great speed. To the east of the City, the White Tower, symbol of Norman domination; then came Baynard's Castle, St. Mary le Bow and Montfichet's Tower. To the west, St. Paul's was completely rebuilt.

It was not until 1090 that Alfune, then Bishop of London, founded the Norman church of St. Giles, a new stone church, which, it is thought, may have been built on the site of a small Saxon chapel lying just outside the wall, close to Cripplegate. Thirty-three years later, Alfune helped and advised Rahere over the founding of a priory church and hospital, dedicated to St. Bartholomew, in Smithfield.

During the twelfth century the area begins to come to life. A horse-fair was held at Smithfield every Friday, and, once a year, the noisy "Cloth" fair erupted for three days near the new St. Bartholomew's church. There was a special burying-ground which had been set aside for the Jewish community, north of Aldersgate.

If the winter was particularly cold, and the marsh north of the wall had frozen over, young men from the City flocked out to skim across the ice and fall about on improvised skates. Buildings went up, and often burned down again. People drank too much — a weakness encouraged by the large number of brewers who were beginning to settle in the "suburb without the walls". Money was raised to build a bridge across the Thames and, in

1189, Henry Fitzailwyn became the first Mayor of the City of London.

In 1244 the brewers decided to rebuild the Cripplegate at their own expense: they widened the road running through it and gave greater clearance for vehicles driving underneath. Anne of Lodburie drowned herself in the large pool by St. Giles' church, and King Henry III ordered the City walls to be repaired and kept in better order. In 1282 London shivered through a terrible winter, the frost so severe that five arches of London Bridge collapsed into the river. By now, pigs, wandering freely in the streets and lanes, had become such a nuisance that two men were employed to catch and either kill them or fine their owners 4d.

Part of Smithfield had been a place for executions for some time, and it was there that the Scottish patriot, Sir William Wallace, was executed in 1305. The gates into the City had always been closed at 8pm, when the curfew rang out from St Martin le Grand, but now a sense of insecurity was so great that the "watch" was increased day and night — eight armed men at both Aldersgate and Cripplegate. Huddled outside the wall, to fend for itself as best it could, lay St Giles', with its growing parish, an increasing number of houses, at least nine shops in Golden Lane, five in *La Barbecane* itself, a tannery in Moore Street and a medley of taverns and breweries. Then the nobility began to arrive:

King Edward III, in the year 1336, gave unto Robert Ufford, Earl of Suffolk, by the name of his manor of Base Court, in the parish of St. Giles without Cripplegate of London, commonly called the Barbican. John Stow *1598.*

In November 1348, the Black Death reached London and a huge graveyard was dug where Charterhouse Square now stands, to bury the bodies of thousands of victims. Ten years later, the pestilence forgotten, people stopped work and rushed out to watch the glittering processions of lords and ladies, knights and squires, who came riding through the gates and out into Smithfield. It had become the fashionable place to hold Royal jousts and great tournaments, some lasting for seven days.

At this time a mason, carpenter or plasterer earned on average 6d a day. Hiring a cart to carry a load from Cripplegate to Chepe cost 3d, a man's gown 14d and a pair of shoes (made of cow-leather) 6d. Prices were carefully pegged:

. . . that no cook shall take more for putting a capon or rabbit in a pasty than one penny, on pain of imprisonment.

And punishment for theft was unbelievably harsh: Simon de Berdesdale, of Aldersgate Street, was hanged for stealing two coats valued at twenty-four shillings.

In 1379, when a charge of 5 pence was levied on every householder towards the cost of cleaning the ditch outside the wall, there may well have been some muted mutterings of discontent. Two years later the mutterings became a roar of anger over the poll-tax.

In February 1381, the Barons of the Exchequer were ordered to collect the whole of this new tax. (Earlier attempts had been a failure as the majority of the population made false returns to avoid payment). As soon as a serious effort was made to collect the money, violence broke out. In June, Wat Tyler led an "army" of tax rebels from Kent towards London. They crossed London Bridge and, joined by men from Essex and Hertfordshire, pillaged Lambeth Palace, destroyed the Savoy and both Fleet and Newgate prisons and murdered — among others — the Archbishop, Simon of Sudbury.

Preliminary negotiations having failed, the fourteen year old king, Richard II, invited Wat Tyler and the rebels to meet him at Smithfield. It was there, in front of the hospital, that the king spoke to the rebel leader. It was there, when Tyler drew his dagger, that the Lord Mayor, William Walworth, assuming an implied threat to the king, cut him down with a cutlass. One of the king's squires then drew his sword and ran Wat Tyler twice through the body in front of the shocked and now silent crowd.

In this tense atmosphere, the King apparently rode forward and, addressing the crowd, told them to follow him to the fields north of Clerkenwell. From there most of them were persuaded to disperse and the rebellion, in London at least, was over.

. . . .

Early in the fifteenth century the City wall was breached north of Coleman Street and a new gate, Moorgate, was built. In 1415 everyone who could walk joined the great, winding procession from the City to Westminster, to attend a thanksgiving service for the victory at Agincourt.

In Cripplegate the first Hall for the Fellowship of Surgeons (later united with the Barbers), was built in Monkwell Street, and a new cistern for storing water was constructed. Taverns continued to open up all over the area (to the satisfaction of what appear to be an unlimited number of patrons), all flaunting beautiful names: *The Hynde on the Hope* in Fore Street, *The Peacock on the Hoop* on the corner of Whitecross Street, *The Flower de Lys* in Golden Lane and *Le Maydenhede and Le Bell* in Moore Street.

Towards the end of the century Thomas More, born in Cripplegate parish, and a pupil at St. Anthony's School in the City, probably joined in enthusiastically on his way home from school, when his friends battled with their rivals from St. Paul's. To the irritation of passers-by, the boys swarmed through the streets, hitting each other about the head with their satchels and exchanging colourful insults.

In 1485, after the brief and uneasy reign of Richard III, Henry VII ascended the throne. The Cripplegate was rebuilt once again, and at Moorfields smallholdings, hovels and orchards were swept away to be replaced by a large field for archery practice. Bow-string makers, fletchers and bowyers immediately began to settle in nearby Grub Street. Although the wall had been repaired, (the stretch between Cripplegate and Aldersgate subsidised by the Goldsmiths), it was beginning to become unnecessary as part of the defensive system of the City. More and more people were moving out to live in the *"suburbs"*, more and more houses and premises were being built — jostling up against the homes of the aristocracy and the religious foundations. As the available land became scarce, so more buildings were crammed into less space — "courts" and "alleys" appeared and the Barbican began to bustle with a rich, varied, noisy and exciting life.

THE
SIXTEENTH
CENTURY

On the north side of this Beech Lane,
towards White Cross Street, the
Drapers of London have lately built
eight Alms Houses of brick and
timber, for eight poor widows of their
own company, whom they have
placed there rent free, according to
the gift of Lady Askew, widow to Sir
Christopher Askew, sometime draper,
and mayor 1533.

John Stow's Survey of London. First
published 1598

THE
SIXTEENTH
CENTURY

*h*enry VIII ascended the throne in 1509. By the time the century ended, his daughter, Elizabeth I had been Queen for over forty years.

It was an age of great magnificence and terrifying religious controversy — of squalor, cruelty and unsurpassed brilliance. It was the age of Shakespeare, Ben Jonson, Inigo Jones and Holbein, of historians, sea captains, adventurers and scholars. It saw the suppression of the monasteries — including Charterhouse Priory — and the torture and execution of men and women for their religious beliefs. Sir Thomas More, now a statesman, scholar and author of *Utopia* (1516), was beheaded in 1535; Anne Askew was burned to death at Smithfield in 1546.

In the area around the Barbican there were improvements. The Moor Fields were drained on the orders of the Lord Mayor, Roger Ashley, and Sir Thomas Seymour had sluices constructed to divert the waters over the old town ditch. Sir William Petre bought land between Little Britain and Long Lane and built himself a large mansion facing onto Aldersgate Street. At the same time, Edward (later Lord) North, who had been granted the Charterhouse, was re-building the old priory into a town house "very grand, with courtyards".

In 1533 Charles Brandon, Duke of Suffolk, aged forty-eight and owner of the manor of Basecourt (known as Barbican), married the very young (and very lively) Catharine Willoughby. The Duke died twelve years later and Catharine married Richard Bertie.

In the streets, lanes and alleys that lay around the homes of the wealthy swarmed

Right:
Section of Ralph Agas' map
(c.1562/3), showing Barbican area.

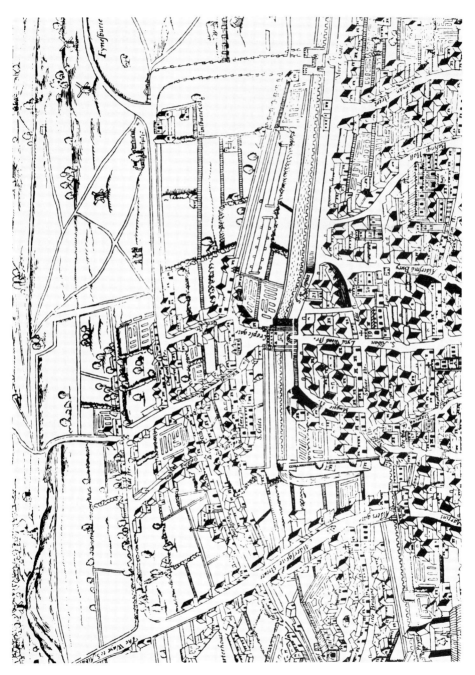

the ordinary people of the area — brewers, gardeners, beggars, bow-makers, actors, haberdashers, thieves, book-sellers, printers, pewterers and prostitutes. In 1534 the living quarters over the Cripplegate were granted to one of the Lord Mayor's officers — with the injunction that he could remain there "as long as he shall well and truly behave himselffe".

After the death of Henry VIII, Catharine Willoughby's eldest son was chosen to carry the orb at Edward VI's coronation. A committed and spirited Protestant, Catharine had taken great delight in tormenting Bishop Gardiner, intransigent supporter of the old religion. Once, laughing, she had chosen to sit by him at dinner "as the man she loved least". Later, adding injury to insult, she had mocked him by calling her pet dog 'Gardiner' and carrying it with her on a public occasion, dressed in miniature robes.

Stephen Gardiner did not forget her impudence and, when the young king died and Mary Tudor took over the throne, Catharine's husband was summoned and given a chilling warning. In January 1555 Catharine Willoughby slipped secretly away from her home in the Barbican. She fled, disguised, to Leigh in Essex and from there her small party sailed for the coast of Brabant. Eventually she and her husband were offered refuge in Lithuania.

Three years later, in November 1558, Mary Tudor, bitter and disillusioned, died at Lambeth Palace. Her half-sister, the Princess Elizabeth, set off from Hatfield, arriving at Lord North's home in the Charterhouse on the twenty-third. Then, bells ringing, the streets lined with jubilant and noisy crowds:

> On Mondaie the eight and twentieth of November, about two of the clocke in the afternoone, Hir Grace removed againe, and taking her chariot, rode from my Lord North's house alongst the Barbican, and entering by Cripplegate into the citie, kept along the wall to Bishopsgate . . .

The following year Elizabeth rode through the city again — on her way to her coronation — and Catharine Willoughby returned home to the Barbican with her husband.

. . . .

And so the Elizabethan Age began.

John Foxe published his *Actes and Monuments* (better known as *The Book of Martyrs*) and settled in Grub Street. Timothy Penredd, a yeoman of the

A house off Grub Street.

Sir Humphrey Gilbert: died when his ship sank without trace in 1583.

Sir Martin Frobisher: knighted on board ship during the Armada.

parish of Cripplegate, was indicted for forgery and condemned to stand in the pillory for two successive market days. (On the first day one of his ears was nailed to the pillory — the other ear on the second day). Inigo Jones, a clothworker's son, was christened in St Bartholmew The Less and Ambrose Nicholas, Lord Mayor, founded twelve alms-houses in 'Monke's Well Street'.

Sir Humphrey Gilbert of Redcross Street, continually petitioning the Queen to allow him to lead an expedition "for the discovery of a passage by the North West", visited his old friend and neighbour, Martin Frobisher, to discuss his hopes and plans. It was seven long years before the Queen relented but, in June 1583, the expedition finally set sail from Plymouth. By August they had taken possession of Newfoundland. It was some time before his family and friends heard that the smallest ship, the *Squirrel*, carrying Sir Humphrey Gilbert, had sunk without trace during a terrible storm in the Azores.

In 1588 came the year of the Armada — the year that Martin Frobisher, commanding the *Triumph*, was knighted on board during the battle. Nearer home the parishioners of St Giles' welcomed their new vicar, Lancelot Andrewes. A gentle, wise and scholarly man, he stayed with them for sixteen years, moving on to become Bishop of Chichester, then Ely and Winchester.

By now the old 'Cloth' fair was part of a much larger event — Bartholomew Fair, a brawling, sprawling, fourteen-day carnival. Huge crowds came to see the wrestlers, puppet-shows, tight-rope dancing, the exhibiting of wild beasts, dwarfs and monsters, the plays, shooting-competitions and operas. Among them, no doubt, was Ben Jonson.

In 1559 Simon Forman moved into the area. He wrote in his journal :

The 22 dai of Aug I toke a chamber at Jeams Askes in Barbican.

And there, for some years, he practised his own particular mixture of astrology, dubious medical advice and fortune telling. Among his customers came Catharine Willoughby's grand-daughter and Mary Mountjoy of Silver Street, soon to have William Shakespeare lodging at her home. Forman was later implicated in the case of the poisoning of Sir Thomas Overbury.

Towards the end of the century Ben Jonson and his wife Anne were living in Cripplegate parish and their son Joseph was baptised there in 1599. A few years earlier the remains of Sir Martin Frobisher had been carried from Plymouth to be buried in St Giles'. The first edition of John Stow's *Survey of London* was published in 1598, describing the suburb without Cripplegate as containing "more than eighteen hundred householders and above four thousand communicants".

A busy, thriving area in fact — with a growing population and, like the rest of London, with severe traffic problems:

Then the number of cars, drays, carts and coaches, more than hath been accustomed, the streets and lanes being straitened, must needs be dangerous, as daily experience proveth.

THE
SEVENTEENTH
CENTURY

Falstaff: *Where's Bardolf?*
Page: *He's gone into Smithfield*
to buy your worship a horse.

William Shakespeare: Henry IV Part Two

THE SEVENTEENTH CENTURY

a new theatre was going up between Golden Lane and Whitecross Street. The actor Edward Alleyn and his father-in-law Philip Henslowe had bought the land, engaged Peter Street to build the frame and by January 1600 the building was taking shape. It was three storeys high and, unusual for the time, square.

The Fortune Theatre opened that autumn with the usual excitement, fanfare of trumpets, stage-fright and applause. As their first performance The Admiral's Men may well have chosen Dekker's play *Fortune's Tennis*.

For the next twenty years The Fortune presented popular entertainment and serious drama to an eager if somewhat undisciplined audience. It was not very long before Mary Frith, a local cobbler's daughter, was taken to court and confessed to having appeared there dressed in men's clothes and singing lewd songs. Then two butchers, Ralph Brewin and John Linsey, were charged with hurling vulgar abuse at certain 'gentlemen' during a performance.

In 1603 Elizabeth I died and at the Barbican crowds caught a glimpse of her successor, James VI of Scotland, as he rode into the City through Aldersgate. By the following year Ben Jonson had moved away to Blackfriars, the poet Nicholas Breton was living in Redcross Street and William Shakespeare was lodging at the Mountjoys'. Christopher Mountjoy, a tire-maker (a maker of women's headdresses), lived with his family in a house on the corner of Silver and Monkwell Street. Shakespeare's *Othello* was soon to be given a command performance at the Ban-

Mary Frith (alias Moll Cutpurse), who sang 'lewd songs' at the Fortune Theatre.

queting Hall in Whitehall and the first quarto of *Hamlet* had recently been published by Nicholas Ling and a young stationer, called John Trundle, working in the Barbican. This particular quarto of *Hamlet* was later named the 'bad' quarto as it was a pirated and incomplete version of the play.*

. . . .

In 1615, in a worthy attempt to create an orderly and peaceful market, Smithfield was paved, railings put up and sewers laid down. Then the Aldersgate, having become rather shabby, was pulled down and rebuilt. The traffic, however, was worse than ever and, to the despair of those in authority, people continued to behave in a generally untidy, rude and uproarious way. There had been another stabbing incident at the Fortune and the public punishment of several local brothel-keepers seemed to make very little difference to the popularity of their trade. Among hundreds of other cases, a carter was taken to court, much the worse for wear, and accused of creating a nuisance by staggering up and down Whitecross Street and shouting insults at all the women he passed "in a drunken and tumultuous manner".

Not many people were particularly interested when an unknown young man called Oliver Cromwell married Elizabeth Bourchier at St Giles Cripplegate in 1620. There was more to gossip about the following year when their local theatre was burned down:

"On Sonday night here was a great fire at the Fortune in Golden-Lane, the fayrest

John Speed: published a series of fifty-four 'Maps of England and Wales' (1608/1610).

*(It is interesting to speculate as to whether John Trundle was connected with the pirating of Shakespeare's masterpiece!)

play-house in this town. It was quite burnt downe in two houres & all their apparell & play-bookes lost, wherby those poore companions are quite undone".

With this fire, although The Fortune was rebuilt, the last vestiges of the Elizabethan age began to fade. Shakespeare was now dead, Ben Jonson ageing and John Speed, Merchant Taylor, historian, cartographer (and father of eighteen children), soon buried in St Giles'.

. . . .

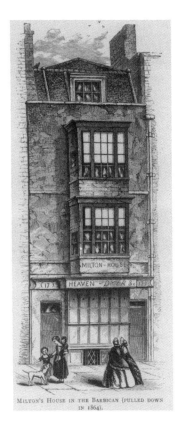

MILTON'S HOUSE IN THE BARBICAN (PULLED DOWN IN 1864).

Charles I began his reign in 1625. It was a reign that started uneasily, developed into civil war and ended with the King's execution. During these years John Milton lived in Barbican Street, a few doors away from the home of the elderly scholar Sir Henry Spelman. The Barber-Surgeons made good use of their new Anatomical Theatre designed by Inigo Jones and more and more book-sellers and printers set up business in the area.

The King was executed at Whitehall in 1649 and the same year the inside of The Fortune Theatre was destroyed by soldiers and left a shell. Mary Frith (known as Moll Cutpurse), who had once sung lewd songs there, died and, her colourful criminal career over, was buried in St Bride's, Fleet Street.

During the Commonwealth, while Oliver Cromwell was Lord General and then Lord Protector, John Milton (now Latin Secretary to the new Council of State), began work again on an early draft of *Paradise Lost*. Petre

House, in Aldersgate Street, was turned into a prison and the parishioners of St Alphage, London Wall, chose Thomas Doolittle as their vicar. Young and enthusiastic, he was one of many non-conformists who were beginning to move into the area, not all of them as popular as Dr Doolittle.

In 1658, the year Cromwell died, Samuel Annesley was presented as the new vicar at St Giles Cripplegate. His parishioners listened carefully to his first sermon and later, led by the Earl of Bridgewater, promptly signed a petition requesting his removal:

Dr Ansley (they said) *doth possesse the said Vicaridge contrary to the votes and desires of the inhabitants of the said parish who were altogether ignorant how he came to possess the same.*

Lauderdale House: home of John Maitland Duke of Lauderdale.

Samuel Annesley sat it out at St. Giles' for a few years and then resigned, moving to Bishopsgate to open a chapel.

. . . .

In a welter of cheers, bells, enthusiasm and relief, Charles II ascended the throne in 1660 and the monarchy was restored. John Milton slipped quietly into obscurity for a while and Daniel Foe (later Defoe), a butcher's son, was born in Fore Street. John Maitland, Duke of Lauderdale, one of the King's ministers, came and went importantly from his home in the Barbican, and the King himself paid a visit to Prince Rupert, now an elderly Cavalier living in Beech Lane. After nine years at St. Alphage, Thomas Doolittle left to open a boarding school at Moorfields. His assistant, Thomas Vincent, another nonconformist, had been minister at a church in Milk Street.

Apart from an apprentices' riot in 1664, nothing greatly disturbed the hurly-burly of existence in Cripplegate parish. Noise and dirt were taken for granted. Over-crowding, on a grand scale, was a fact of life. Then came the nightmare:

> "A dreadful plague in London was
> In the year sixty-five,
> Which swept an hundred thousand souls
> Away; yet I alive."
>
> *Daniel Defoe*

Nobody had the slightest idea of what was in store. Over the years they had learned to live with outbreaks of the Plague — it came and went, they prayed — and then forgot. And so, when Philip Puller's wife died in Chiswell Street on June 2nd, people were not particularly surprised . . . Then John Barker, a weaver of Old Street . . . well, poor man!

By the end of the month it was a different matter altogether. Those who could were packing up, closing their homes and leaving hurriedly for the country. Among them went Dr. Pritchett, Vicar of St. Giles'. His curate and the parish clerk, Thomas Luckeyne and Nicholas Pyne, remained to cope as best they could. The summer grew hot and still.

August 18th 1665 — facsimile of details from St. Giles' Burial Register.

August 1665

Anne dau: of Roberta Chamberlin wid	Convul below	18
Elizab Rolph wid	yplagu below	18
Anne wife of Charles Ingo distiller	yplagu below	15
Anne wife of Christopher Dudson Cooper	yplagu Above	15
Elizab Larkin serv to Mary Emmory wid	yplagu Above	18
John son of James Lamb weauer	yplagu Above	18
John son of John Masters glouer	ffeauer Above	18
Mary Cripplegate a parish child	tooth Above	18
Anne dau: of ye Peter Dod tailer	yplague Above	18
Elizab wife of Edmond Harding porter	yplague Above	18
Elizab dau: of Eliz: Seaman wid	yplague Above	18
Elizab Carpenter	yplague Above	18
Benj: son of [ ] Crowder	yplague Above	15
Gilbert Skelton Carman	yplague below	18
Thomas Hunt Smith	yplague Above	18
Thomas Lorbee Currier	yplague Above	18
Willm son of [ ] Watkins porter	yplague Above	18
Mary dau: of Willm Andrews butcher	Sto: Sto: Above	18
Barnard Crow bricklayer	Spotfea below	18
Quartorne dau: of wid Gilman	teeth Above	18
Anne serv to Mr Tailor butcher	Spotfea Above	18
Marg wife of Tho: ffloid Seaman	ffeauer below	18
Anne dau: of John Snow	yplague Above	1.
Anne dau: of Stephen ypottinger porter	Gri: guk Above	1.
Siluanus Bartlet weauer	yplague Above	18

In July, entries for burials in St. Giles' register book filled seventy one pages. Orders published by the Lord Mayor and Aldermen were acted upon immediately:

— ". . . that special care be taken that no stinking fish, or unwholesome flesh, or musty corn . . . be suffered to be sold about the city."

— ". . . that the dogs be killed by the dog-killers appointed for that purpose."

— ". . . that every house visited be marked with a red cross of a foot long in the middle of the door . . . and with these usual printed words, that is to say 'Lord have mercy upon us'."

It was too late. People fell sick hourly, and by August the horror had reached its peak. In one day alone, St. Giles' buried a hundred and fifty-one of its parishioners and

Burying the dead during the Plague of 1665. contemporary woodcut.

over eight hundred died in a week; "Now Death rides triumphantly on his pale horse through our streets", wrote Thomas Vincent. There were scenes of unbearable suffering — but when Edward Smallie, of Hoxton, who had rescued three small children from Whitecross Street, refused to return them, he was committed to stand for trial.

Painfully slowly, the number of deaths began to decrease and it was only towards the end of September that the full effect became clear. John Tillson of St. Paul's, in a letter to a friend, commented:

I am sure that the miserable condition of St. Giles' Cripplegate . . . is more to be pitied than any parish in London.

Nicholas Pyne, the parish clerk, had continued to keep the appalling records until he too died. Eventually it was estimated that the Plague had killed almost eight thousand in the area.

. . . .

In September 1666, only eight months after people had begun to return to the Barbican and attempt to rebuild their lives, the City of London was devastated once again:

September 2nd: This fatal night, about ten, began the deplorable fire, near Fish Street . . .

John Evelyn

Although the Great Fire started to the east of the City, it spread swiftly and, fanned by the wind, moved westward totally out of control:

All the skie was of a fiery aspect, like the top of a burning oven, and the light seene above 40 miles round for many nights. God grant mine eyes may never behold the like.

People fled, panicking, onto the Thames in boats and away from buildings to the nearest open spaces. Moorfields became a huge refugee camp with thousands huddled in makeshift tents, clutching their children and any precious possessions they could carry.

A section of Ogilby & Morgan's map (1677) showing Barbican area.

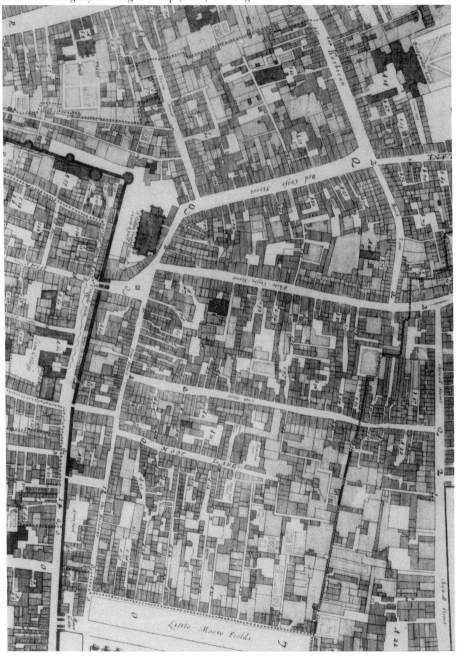

Through Cornhill, down Cheapside, St. Paul's ablaze, licking northwards earer and nearer to Smithfield and Cripplegate. The Lord Mayor ordered houses to be pulled down, the King ordered bread to be distributed to the homeless, and Samuel Pepys walking to Moorfields, scorched the soles of his shoes on the "red hot coals".

By Friday, the seventh, it was over. The City had been laid waste but most of the Barbican and St. Giles' parish had escaped. St. Olave's, Silver Street, had been destroyed, so had the Barber-Surgeons' Hall. Some houses in Fore Street had been blown up to prevent the fire spreading, but only the windows of St. Giles' church had been damaged by the extreme heat.

. . . .

Rebuilding began everywhere, and, only two years after the Great Fire, Samuel Pepys and his friend Harris, came to look at the "Chryurgeon's Hall, where they are building it new very fine". Pepys also visited the recently-established stage school for children, (nicknamed, "The Nursery"), in Golden Lane, and saw there a tragedy called, "Jeronimo is mad again." He was less than complimentary:

> . . . the house is better and the music better than we looked for, and the acting not much worse, because I expected as bad as could be.

Over the next thirty years, various brawls and riots disturbed the Barbican area, following the pattern of the whole country. Weavers in Moorfields and Cloth Fair, afraid that the new engine-looms would put them out of work, joined the violent demonstrations of 1675. Politics moved into a new age as a two party system began to emerge and the differences between "Whigs" and "Tories" were often settled in the streets — in 1681 a group of Tories hid in Charterhouse Yard and leapt out to ambush a procession of Whigs marching along Aldersgate.

Bethlehem Hospital for "lunatics", (known to everyone as Bedlam), moved from Bishopsgate to Moorgate, the new building designed by Robert Hooke, costing £17,000. Petre House in Aldersgate Street was handed over to the Bishop of London and re-named London House, and fire — always a hazard — destroyed the Earl of Bridgewater's home, killing two of his children. After the revocation of the Edict of Nantes, large numbers of immigrant French protestants, Huguenots, arrived to settle in the area.

The poet John Milton as a young man.

John Milton died in 1674. He had been living in Artillery Row, (now Bunhill Row), for many years and it was there that he completed *Paradise Lost* (1667) and wrote *Paradise Regained* (1671). He was buried in St. Giles' Cripplegate, the entry in the register reading: "John Milton, Gentleman, Consumption, 12" (November). Seven years later the stone marking his grave was taken away, a fact noted by John Aubrey in his inimitable style:

His stone is now removed: about two years since, the two steppes to the communion table were raysed. I ghesse Jo. Speed and he lie together.

The Thames froze in 1683 and Londoners diverted themselves on the solid ice covered with stalls, shops, booths and even a printing press. Over the next few years, extremes in the weather — heavy frosts in the winters, long droughts in the summer — became almost commonplace. On January 11th 1690, John Evelyn wrote:

This night there was a most extraordinary storm of wind . . . it did great harm in many places, blowing down houses, trees etc., killing many people. It began about two in the morning . . .

John Bunyan, author of *Pilgrim's Progress* (1678) who had preached several times in the Barbican area, died in 1688 and was buried in Bunhill Fields. In November 1697, William Hogarth was born in Bartholomew Close and christened in St. Bartholomew the Great.

In November 1699 a thick fog blanketed the whole of London. Coughing and spluttering — losing their way in familiar streets and alleys — people in the Barbican groped their way home, and into the eighteenth century.

THE
EIGHTEENTH
CENTURY

The Tiger in Bartholomew Fair,
that yesterday gave such
satisfaction to persons of all qualities
by pulling the feathers so nicely
from live fowls will, at the request
of several persons, do the same
this day; price 6d each.

[Advertisement in "The Postman To
Tuesday" Sept 1701]

THE EIGHTEENTH CENTURY

*t*he early part of the eighteenth century saw little change in the Barbican area. Bartholomew Fair continued, colourful, noisy, often crude, sometimes terrifying — always entertaining. Having avoided the worst of the Great Fire, the streets, lanes, courts and alleys remained, with many of the old Elizabethan houses dilapidated but still intact. Gradually, as the wealthy began to move away to less crowded districts, these buildings were divided into tenements or replaced with small houses. The population increased — and so did poverty.

Moorfields was much admired for the improvements that were made — gardens laid out with beautiful and well-maintained 'walks'. Queen Anne came to the throne and, at last, Sir Christopher Wren's new St Paul's was completed. St Giles' began an extensive programme of repairs and alterations and St Luke's in Old Street was built, to take over a portion of the over-burdened parish.

Religious controversy burned as fiercely as ever — Daniel Defoe published *The Shortest Way with Dissenters* in 1702. He was promptly clapped into the pillory for his pains and then transferred to Newgate Prison, where he began to write his (thrice-weekly) paper, *The Review*. Thomas Doolittle "Last of the London Ejected Clergy" died in 1707 and was buried in Bunhill Fields. Daniel Williams, another well-known dissenting minister, was buried there a few years later, leaving his collection of books to form one of the earliest of London's libraries open to the public in Redcross Street.

In 1714, the year Queen Anne died, a small boy called John Wesley started school at the Charterhouse; William Hogarth, whose family had moved to Long Lane, was serving his apprenticeship to an engraver and, in one of the alleys close to St Giles', Jonathan Wild and his mistress had recently set up "a notorious establishment much frequented by thieves and prostitutes".

This establishment was in fact a 'cover' for an amazing criminal enterprise, master-minded by Jonathan Wild, which specialised in the receiving — and selling back at an inflated price — of stolen property.

Wild soon moved from the Barbican to Holborn where, now outwardly respectable, he succeeded in duping his victims for another ten years. Caught at last in 1725, he was committed to Newgate, tried, executed and, or so everyone said, portrayed as Mr. Peachum in John Gay's *The Beggar's Opera*.

Meanwhile an Act of Common Council had been passed "for lighting streets, lanes, courts and alleys of the City of London and liberties thereof". William Hogarth, issuing a shop card, opened a business as an engraver from his mother's house in Long Lane and 'Old Nan', an eighteenth century 'bag-lady' was buried at St. Giles' by the company of Exeter Change (at her death £500 had been found in a trunk in her 'hovel').

In 1731 Daniel Defoe, journalist and author of *Robinson Crusoe* and *A Tour Through The Whole Island Of Great Britain*, died "of lethargy" at his rooms in Ropemaker Alley. He was buried in Bunhill Fields.

Towards the middle of the century other personalities began to emerge. John Wesley, now in his twenties, returned to the district and in May 1738 wrote the well-known passage referring to his conversion:

In the evening I went very unwillingly to a society in Aldersgate Street, where one was reading Luther's preface to the Epistle to the Romans. About a quarter before nine, while he was describing the change which God works in the heart through faith in Christ, I felt my heart strangely warmed . . .

Wesley preached at Moorfields in a disused building called 'The Foundery' and became a familiar sight riding through the Barbican on horseback.

Two other men, Samuel Whitbread and George Seddon, also moved into the area. In 1750 Samuel Whitbread bought the King's Head brewery in Chiswell Street and, a few years later, George Seddon, Master Cabinet Maker, established a furniture business on a site which included London House in Aldersgate Street. They were both hugely successful. By 1787 Samuel Whitbread's brewery was so well-known that George III and Queen Charlotte paid an official visit and were taken to admire the ten horse-power steam engine recently installed for grinding the malt and raising water.

George Seddon's business gradually became a furniture 'emporium', the largest furniture-making firm in London. Sophie von la Roche, a German tourist, shown round in 1786, wrote:

London House — George Seddon's furniture emporium.

We drove first to Mr Seddon's, a cabinet-maker. He employs four hundred apprentices on any work connected with the making of household furniture . . . all these are housed in a building with six wings. In the basement mirrors are cast and cut — charming dressing-tables are also to be seen . . . chintz . . . silk and wool material . . . carpets. In short anything one might desire to furnish a house. Seddon seemed to me a respectable man, a man of genius, too, with an understanding for the needs of the needy and luxurious.

Not that this had been achieved without some major set-backs. In 1768 a severe fire caused extensive damage to George Seddon's property and he discovered to his horror that he had allowed his policy at the Sun Insurance Office to lapse. His petition for aid, claiming losses of £7,700, gained him only £500.

Although both businesses provided much needed employment this was a drop in the ocean compared to an area where overcrowding and wretched poverty were an increasing problem. The parish authorities and the Vestry of St Giles' struggled to fulfil their responsibilities but it was often a losing battle. In 1765 the church decided to employ two people during Divine Service "to prevent noises and disturbances usually made by boys and beggars".

Iron spikes were also placed on the doors opening on to the middle aisle, this time "to prevent boys from climbing over the same".

The anti-catholic 'Gordon Riots' burst explosively into the Barbican in June 1780. Inflamed by religious bigotry, by petty grudges, by drink and by resentment, an angry mob went berserk. Catholics were not only abused and insulted, their homes were broken into, their goods and furniture smashed and burned. Father Dillon, priest of a small chapel in Ropemaker Alley, was dragged from his bed and badly beaten. In Golden Lane a pawnbroker saw his house destroyed and a nearby tavern was torn down. The riots continued throughout London for seven days.

. . . .

Four years later on September 15th 1784, their differences quite forgotten, residents of the Barbican had only one ambition. Whoever they were and wherever they lived they were determined to catch a glimpse of The Balloon which, they had heard, would float up into the sky from the artillery ground in Chiswell Street. Few believed another rumour — that a Mr Lunardi would actually go up with it.

Vincent Lunardi, secretary to the Neapolitan Ambassador, was indeed about to accomplish this feat. He intended to take a pigeon, a cat, a dog and a Mr Biggin with him. Unfortunately it took rather a long time to fill the balloon and the crowd, suspecting a practical joke, grew impatient and then rather unpleasant. Lunardi decided to leave immediately. He climbed into the gallery and, discharging part of the ballast — including Mr Biggin — gave the signal for lift-off. Later describing these first few moments he wrote:

As a multitude lay before me of a hundred and fifty thousand people, who had not seen my ascent from the ground, I had recourse to every stratagem to let them know I was in the gallery and they literally rent the air with their acclamations and applause.

Filled with hydrogen, the huge balloon floated slowly up and away from Chiswell Street, over the Barbican and off into the distance over St. Paul's. The pigeon escaped quite quickly and Lunardi had to make a temporary landing at South Mimms to leave the shivering cat. He and the dog finally brought the journey to a triumphant conclusion at Standon, near Ware in Hertfordshire . . . it had taken them two and a quarter hours.

Far right:
Lunardi's balloon leaving the
Honourable Artillery Ground in
September 1784.

Towards the end of the century there was some evidence of change. The poverty, the crumbling over-crowded Elizabethan mansions, the teeming alleys, were still there, but six underground cisterns had been built for the brewery in Chiswell Street. The old gates at Cripplegate and Aldersgate had gone and the Metropolitan Dispensary and Charitable Fund was established in Fore Street. Some of the patients from 'Bedlam' were moved to a new hospital in Old Street and a bust of John Milton (after a rather bizarre search for his coffin), was donated by Samuel Whitbread and placed in St. Giles' church.

Alice Hepplewhite of Redcross Street, widow of George Hepplewhite, a cabinet and chair maker, took a folio of her husband's designs to be published — and so, unknowingly, gave her husband's name to a particular style of eighteenth century English furniture. Two young men, Edward Lowe and William Jobbins, were sentenced to death for deliberately setting fire to Mr Gilding's house in Aldersgate Street and, in March 1791, ten thousand people filed past John Wesley's coffin at the chapel in City Road. Four years later, John Keats, son of a prosperous livery stable owner, was born at Moorgate.

As the eighteenth century ended, George III was still on the Throne and William Pitt the Younger was Prime Minister. The population of Cripplegate Ward was now over eleven thousand.

Far right:
A corner of St Giles' churchyard.
Drawn by J. T. Smith in 1793.

THE
NINETEENTH
CENTURY

*They had crossed Smithfield together,
and Clenman was left alone at the
corner of Barbican.*

Charles Dickens: *Little Dorrit*

THE NINETEENTH CENTURY

*d*uring this century, people living in the Barbican were to witness major changes and the population dropped from over fourteen thousand to two thousand.

At first life continued much as usual. The chiming machine in St. Giles' church continued to play its seven tunes — one for each day of the week:

Sunday	"Easter Hymn"
Monday	"National Anthem"
Tuesday	"Auld Lang Syne"
Wednesday	"Hanover"
Thursday	"Hark! 'tis the bells"
Friday	"Mariners' Hymn"
Saturday	"Home, sweet home"

Well-known local figures died — George Seddon in 1801 and, a little later, the popular Swiss physician Dr. Francis Joseph Pahus de Valangin, who had practised in Fore Street for thirty-five years. A great many of the tortuous courts and alleys in the Jewin Street area off Aldersgate were demolished and replaced by Jewin Crescent, which boasted a surgeon, several jewellers, a brass foundry and a Welsh chapel where the services were held in Welsh. "Bedlam" hospital moved away to Lambeth and a Debtors' Prison was built in Whitecross Street.

In 1819, Richard Lambert Jones was elected Common Councilman for Cripplegate Ward and soon began his campaign for a new Library at Guildhall, (eventually sitting on the Library Committee for nineteen years). The following year the Barbican buzzed with excitement at the news that Arthur Thistlewood had been arrested at Mrs Harris's lodging house just off Fore Street. Thistlewood was said to be the ringleader of the Cato Street conspirators who had plotted to assassinate Cabinet Ministers and so overthrow the government.

Queen Victoria began her reign in 1837. The Albion Tavern in Aldersgate Street, famous for its food and wine, became a popular haunt of publishers, and Charles Dickens wrote *Martin Chuzzlewit* (1843), in which Tom Pinch tried to find his way across London.

> *... So on he went, looking up all the streets he came near, and going up half of them; and thus, by dint of not being true to Goswell Street, and filing off into Aldermanbury, and bewildering himself in Barbican ... he found himself, at last, hard by the Monument.*

Then, in the eighteen-fifties, an Act of Parliament was passed which moved the live cattle market away from Smithfield — and the railways began to make their presence felt. The Barbican would never be the same again.

For a while, Smithfield lay empty, a few tawdry stalls appearing once a year in a sad travesty of Bartholomew Fair. In 1868, the new Metropolitan Meat Market, designed by Horace Jones, was opened by the Lord Mayor with great pomp, glittering ceremony and a banquet for one thousand two hundred guests.

> *Three thousand yards of gas-piping fed a number of candelabra and a centre starlight. There were four carvers, in Guildhall dignity, who, mounted on high pedestals, carved barons of beef and boars' heads. The Lord Mayor's footmen shone in gold lace, and the City trumpeter and toastmaster also dignified the feast.*

The magnificent new market was an immediate success, with a turnover of 127,981 tons of produce during the first year, and fierce competition for any of the shops when they became vacant.

During the same period, five new railway termini were built in the City and the railway companies began to buy up any property they could lay their hands on. Old buildings in and around the Barbican began to disappear. *The Swan With Two Necks* tavern, five hundred years old, was one of the first to go, followed by Dr. Williams' Library in Redcross Street, which was closed and transferred to Queen Square, Bloomsbury. The Midland Railway bought the site of the Debtors' prison in Whitecross Street to build a goods depot, and the Metropolitan — about to extend their line from Farringdon to Moorgate — took up premises in Little Moorgate.

Number seventeen, Barbican Street, said to have been John Milton's house, was demolished in 1864, replaced not by a railway office but by one of the hundreds of warehouses that were also springing up all over the area. Barbican Street in fact presented a strange medley of businesses at this time including, in the early days, Mr. Langham's stables, with their "spacious and convenient yards and sheds", a pub called *The Still* at No. 6, soon closed and auctioned off, and the gold and silver refining firm of W. Bryer and Sons at No. 54, with John Bryer's business as a "chronometer maker" next door.

As the railways and warehouses moved in, so the residents began to move out. In 1851 the population of Cripplegate Ward was 14,361. Only thirty years later, in 1881, it had dropped to 4,737. On the other hand, while the numbers actually living there rapidly diminished, so the figures for those coming in to work during the day rose to dizzy heights. By 1891, when the local population was a mere 2000, it was estimated that over 21,000 were actually employed in the area.

In spite of the massive exodus there were still enough people to justify some new "social" building. Cripplegate Ward Boys School was built in Bridgewater Square in 1870, and in 1896 the lovingly planned and designed Cripplegate Institute was opened, providing a library and space for lectures, classes and performances in its theatre. Poverty was still very much in evidence and, while helping to set up a "mission" in Golden Lane

The premises of W. Bryer & Sons, Barbican Street.

in the eighteen-seventies, G. Holden Pike wrote this vivid description of the inhabitants of the Golden Lane and Whitecross Street area:

. . . 30% are costermongers and itinerant street traders; 20% are labourers and poor women who live by washing, charing and needlework; 30% are either paupers or persons of doubtful occupation; and the remaining 20% are industriously wearing out their lives in the attempt to earn a livelihood at the following occupations: — artificial flower makers, hose-sewing at twopence per dozen pairs, toymakers, wood-choppers and crossing-sweepers, gutter-searchers for cigar ends, bone-pickers and dustbin searchers for doctors' bottles which, when washed, are sold to chemists at one shilling and ninepence per gross.

. . . .

The Barbican may have escaped the Great Fire of 1666. At the end of the nineteenth century it was not so fortunate. The warehouses and sweatshops of the day, which included "Australian and other Colonial merchants and dealers in soft goods", were a dangerously high fire risk and in 1897 the "Great Cripplegate Fire" started in an ostrich-feather warehouse near Jewin Street. Huge smoke-clouds settled over the Barbican as the fire spread through the narrow streets and alleys to Redcross Street. By the time it had been brought under control, one hundred and twenty-eight warehouses and small businesses had been destroyed, several thousand people put out of work, and St. Giles' church badly damaged.

THE TWENTIETH CENTURY

City
When the great bell
BOOMS
Over the Portland stone urn,
And from the carved cedar wood
Rises the odour of incense,
I SIT DOWN
In St. Botolph Bishopsgate Churchyard
And wait for the spirit of my grandfather
Toddling along from the Barbican.

John Betjeman

THE
TWENTIETH
CENTURY

*b*y 1901 both the old Lady Eleanor Holles School in Redcross Street and the new Cripplegate boys' school in Bridgewater Square had closed. The number of residents in Cripplegate Ward had fallen to 1,052 but this was probably a matter of complete indifference to the twenty thousand or so who travelled in to the area every day. Large warehouses, small businesses, shops of every description, a fire station, pubs, banks and cafés lined the streets and the Metropolitan Railway divided this hive of activity into two. Horse-sales were still held in premises off Barbican Street and in Whitecross Street the stalls of the open market did a brisk trade to jostling crowds during the lunch hour. St. Giles' churchyard provided some welcome peace and quiet although the chiming machine, now over a hundred years old, still played its daily rota of tunes.

When Britain declared war on Germany on August 4th 1914, territorials of the 8th City of London Battalion were en route for their summer camp at Eastbourne. Trains carrying them there were immediately halted and turned around and for days their headquarters at Bunhill Row — shared with the London Rifle Brigade — was besieged by recalled reservists and eager young volunteers. During the war Bridgewater Square was turned into a market garden where vegetables were grown for the war effort and the Port of London Authority cold store was built in Smithfield.

Not long after the end of the war there were only six hundred and thirty-three people living in Cripplegate Ward. At night and

Far right:
A section of Stanford's map (1914), showing Barbican area.

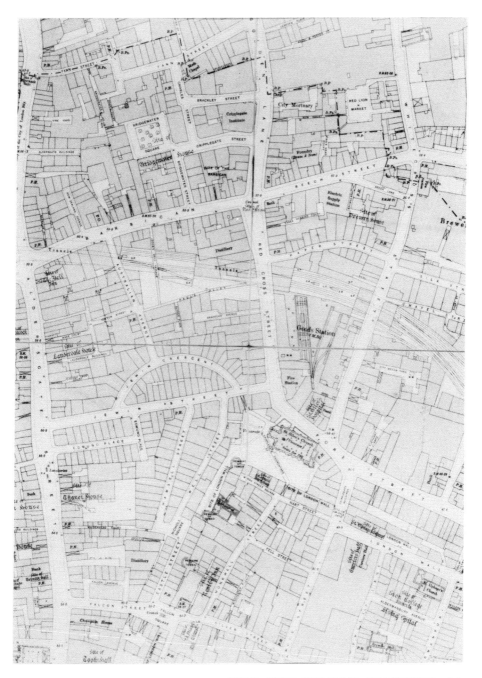

on Sundays the area was almost deserted, a strangely quiet ghost-town, the empty streets waiting for the hordes of commuters to bring them to life the following morning.

One of these commuters, a resident now living in the Barbican, describes the area during the day:

My office was directly opposite St. Giles' church at the corner of Whitecross Street.

In this small area were busy warehouses, shops and small manufacturers, mostly in haberdashery or similar trades. The narrow streets were full of people, clerks, travellers, bank messengers, but above all there was the pervading smell of the brewery just up the road. I shall never forget this smell, mingled with the smell of horses and the wonderful odours from Branch's eating house next door.

Whitecross Street was, as it still is, a busy market, but the lower part was used almost entirely by the Railway as a goods and loading yard and the street was jammed with carts, vans and drays.

In June 1939 a fire broke out in Barbican Street. Eight buildings were soon ablaze and the next day the *Daily Herald* reported severe damage — and the amazing escape of some girls who had been trapped in a cul-de-sac.

In September of that year Britain declared war on Germany.

. . . .

Far right:
Aftermath — Aldersgate Street, looking towards Barbican, 1940.

The first bomb to fall on the City of London landed on the corner of Fore Street and

Wood Street in August 1940, knocking Milton's statue in St. Giles' churchyard off its pedestal and damaging the church tower. Four months later, early in the evening of December 29th, the distant throb of approaching bombers heralded a major raid on the City and the total devastation of the Barbican.

For over three hours incendiary bombs rained down on Cannon Street, the Tower of London, Cheapside, the Guildhall — but particularly over the area between Moorgate and Aldersgate. At first, attempts were made to stop the fires spreading but as the night wore on streets became impassable and some areas had to be left to burn themselves out.

The next morning passengers emerging from Moorgate station stood in blank amazement. There, across a no man's land of rubble and the smouldering remains of buildings, stood St. Paul's. The Cathedral had, against all odds, survived, but St. Giles' church was a shell, the Barber-Surgeons' Hall destroyed, the Central Telegraph Office, the shops, pubs, warehouses and small businesses all gone. The Ironmongers' Hall off Aldersgate Street had been saved by the heroic efforts of the staff who, using stirrup pumps and carrying water, prevented the building from catching fire. By some fluke, the Fire Station in Redcross Street was still standing and sections of the old City wall were now clearly visible.

No further damage was possible to the Barbican itself. In 1944 a flying bomb fell on Bartholomew Close, destroying the Butchers' Hall, and the following year the last bomb to fall on the City of London hit the north-west corner of Smithfield Market, killing a hundred and fifty people.

For several years the Barbican was deserted, a waste-land. Wild flowers, grass and shrubs began to soften the outlines of destruction, birds nested on ledges of broken buildings and pigeons flew in and out through the shattered church. In her novel, *The World my Wilderness*, written at the time, Rose Macaulay traces the relationship of two adolescents, Raoul and Barbary, who meet regularly in the area and explore the ruins of St. Giles:

"They went round outside the church. On the front porch a notice said *"The church is open for Private Prayer and Devotion every Week Day from 10am till 4pm. Saturdays 10am till 1pm. Entrance in Fore Street"*. The door was locked. From the green garden of weeds and gravestones outside the west wall, they scrambled on to a window ledge and dropped down inside the church. It was windy and bare; the iron spokes and wire gauze in the empty windows flapped to and fro. They went into the belfry tower; eight great bronze bells lay broken on the floor by a bronze statue of a man with long hair and high boots. Torn fragments of hymn-books littered the floor . . ."

Rose Macaulay: *The World My Wilderness. 1950*

In April 1947 Dr. Holden and Professor Holford, Joint Consultants on Reconstruction in the City of London, presented their final report to the Improvements and Town Planning Committee of the Corporation. In July, taking advantage of a unique opportunity, W. F. Grimes, Professor of Archaeology at the University of London, began the first archaeological cuttings in the Barbican area. His programme, covering much of the City, had been initiated and organised by the

The scene prior to reconstruction.

Society of Antiquaries of London and was carried out over the next fifteen years. Among many important and exciting finds came the proof that there had been a Roman military fort on the Cripplegate site.

While this vital link, spanning almost 2,000 years of history, was being made, the future of the Barbican was under scrutiny and the complex ritual of "Proposals for Redevelopment", "Alternative Plans", "Motions", "Reports", "Definitions", "Debates", "Instructions", "Consultations", "Recommendations" and "Policies" began.

In 1955, Chamberlin, Powell and Bon, Architects (who had won the competition for the design of the Golden Estate in 1952),

The Barbican site in 1962.

produced a preliminary study of the feasibility of a residential area within the Barbican. The study, accompanied by a model, was presented in May 1956 and the amazing idea of redeveloping 35 acres of the most commercial land in Britain into a residential estate was properly launched. The debate intensified. Then, the Minister of Housing and Local Government, the Rt. Hon. Duncan Sandys, who had already refused planning permission for a project mainly involving office and commercial development, wrote to the Lord Mayor. It was, everyone agreed later, an "historic" letter, urging them to create, on the ruins of the Barbican:

A genuine residential neighbourhood incorporating schools, shops, open spaces and amenities even if this means foregoing a more remunerative return of the land.

A report by a Special Committee was presented and, on the 19th September 1957, the Court of Common Council resolved to accept the Minister's recommendation. The Barbican Committee, with Eric Wilkins as Chairman, was formed and Chamberlin, Powell and Bon appointed consultants, their final report and scheme-design appearing in 1959. They were then appointed architects and, shortly afterwards, building began.

It was a massive undertaking, an imaginative, courageous and exhilarating gesture. The City Corporation was about to write a completely new page in the Barbican's history.

. . . .

Some commercial buildings were planned on the perimeter of the estate, (Lee House was completed in 1962), but the main scheme for the residential area was to include:
— **Housing:** 2,000 flats, maisonettes and houses for up to 6,000 people.
— **A Hostel** with 200 study-bedrooms and communal facilities.
— **A new building** for the City of London School for Girls.
— **The Barbican Centre** for Arts and Conferences
— **The Guildhall School of Music and Drama**
— **The Museum of London**
— **Public Services Buildings**, including a new Fire Station for the London Fire Brigade
— **A sub-station** for the London Electricity Board
— **Car-parking facilities**

This was the moment when the names of some of the oldest streets in the area, notably Redcross Street, Barbican Street and Jewin Street were to vanish for ever. *Route Eleven* (the new London Wall), was carved through to link Aldersgate with Moorgate and in 1960, looking very small and rather forlorn in the middle of a vast building-site, St. Giles' church was formally reopened.

As work progressed and the Barbican Estate began to take shape there were arguments, some go-slows and one strike so bitter that it attracted the gleeful attention of the media. However, the "Topping-Out" ceremony for the first residential block was held in 1966. "Phase Three", it was announced, was at the halfway stage. Interest in the project revived instantly and in October 1968 *The Architects' Journal* noted:

There are 4,300 people on the waiting list for the 2,100 flats, houses and maisonettes that will make up the Barbican scheme in the City of London, where all the dwellings will be leased at market rents.

Although some residents had moved into Milton Court a little earlier, the official opening of Speed House, the first block of flats to be completed, took place late in 1968. Sir Maurice Laing, Chairman of the main contractors, John Laing Construction Limited, formally handed over to the Rt. Hon. the Lord Mayor, Sir Gilbert Samuel Inglefield and the following year, 1969, people were busily moving into their new homes. The new Barbican Estate, planned with such confidence, built with a mixture of hope, anxiety and controversy, had been born.

. . . .

Later that year Princess Alexandra opened the City of London School for Girls next to St. Giles' church — and Queen Elizabeth, the Queen Mother, opened the rebuilt Barber-Surgeons' Hall in Monkwell Square. Still to come were the Museum of London, the Guildhall School of Music and Drama and the Barbican Arts Centre. Of these three it was the Arts Centre which was to cause the greatest upheaval.

The original intention had been to build a theatre and concert hall for the Guildhall School, which could be used for public performances by visiting orchestras and theatre companies. This idea had been rejected and the alternative of a separate Arts Centre was raised.

In 1964 Anthony Besch, the Opera producer, had reported to the Corporation on this issue. His powerful recommendations included a concert hall seating 2,000 and the involvement of a major orchestra and theatre company. At the same time he wrote exploratory letters to Ernest Fleischmann, General Secretary of the London Symphony Orchestra, and to Peter Hall, then Director of the Royal Shakespeare Company. His report ended:

The project for the Concert Hall and Theatre in the Barbican Area has opened the way to exciting and important developments in the arts. It is greatly to be hoped that the original imaginative conception can now be carried through to a logical and impressive conclusion.

The report was accepted, in principle, but plans grew more and more ambitious — a library, restaurants, an art gallery, greater foyer space, a cinema and conference facilities. In 1970 Henry Wrong, who had been associated with the development of the Lincoln Centre in New York and the National Arts Centre in Ottawa, was appointed Administrator of the Centre.

The Arts world stirred in anticipation, but the problems were immense and it soon became clear that the future of the Centre hung in the balance. Feelings ran high, people took sides and pressure groups were formed. The week before a crucial debate at Guildhall, the Evening Standard ran the headline, ***"BUILD OUR ARTS CENTRE NOW!"***

On April 15th 1971, after a fiercely fought debate lasting over four hours, the Barbican Arts Centre project was finally agreed by 78 to 59 votes and building began that year. Some residents, irritated by the continuous noise and dust, viewed the deep excavations and slow progress with a jaundiced eye. The Estate was suffering from growing pains and, in 1974, newspapers reported unrest among tenants, caused by rent increases.

In 1976 the Museum of London, an amalgamation of the older "Guildhall" and "London" museums, opened on the south-west corner of the Barbican. It was soon to become one of the most highly respected, as well as one of the most popular of London's museums. In May the following year came the Guildhall School of Music and Drama, fronting on to Silk Street and next door to the unfinished Arts Centre which was taking longer, and costing rather more, than anyone had expected.

Finally, in March 1982, Her Majesty the Queen, accompanied by the Lord Mayor Sir Christopher Leaver and a delighted Henry Wrong, formally declared the Barbican Centre open in front of an impressive assembly of

Foundation work for the Barbican Centre — 1973.

guests. The London Symphony Orchestra played in the Concert Hall, the Royal Shakespeare Company performed in the Theatre, and the Art Gallery, Library and Conference facilities were duly admired. At the end of the evening residents of the Barbican, standing on their balconies, on the bridge and in the nearby gardens, watched as a glittering display of fireworks burst over St. Giles' church and the lake. The Barbican was complete at last.

. . . .

Over the years the Estate began to mature as people learned how to live there. From the beginning there had been a number of rich,

Her Majesty Queen Elizabeth II and the Lord Mayor Sir Christopher Leaver — opening ceremony of the Barbican Centre 1982.

David Amies, Barbican Manager.

HM The Queen Mother talking with residents on the lawn during her visit in 1984.

famous and glamorous residents ranging from Benazir Bhutto — later to become Prime Minister of Pakistan, Peter Hall and Fiona Richmond, the former sex symbol, to Norman Tebbit, and stars of *Coronation Street*. But the majority of people living there, as many of them were quick to point out, were "perfectly normal". In 1977, David Amies became the new Manager of the Estate, with the unenviable task of dealing, among other things, with the day-to-day problems (some of them quite ordinary, others rather bizarre), of a disparate, articulate and self-conscious community numbering over four thousand.

Small groups of people with a mutual interest in subjects such as music, languages and history began to meet regularly. The Barbican Horticultural Society was formed in 1980 and began to revolutionise the roof

gardens, patios and miles of window boxes. They also scooped a special event when the Queen Mother, (Patron of the London Gardens Society), visited to plant a tree in the quadrangle. The Barbican (residents) Association had been formed as early as 1970 and was going from strength to strength. A children's playgroup was operational by 1976. Residents were not allowed to have pets but, like their Elizabethan forebears, they found imaginative ways of breaking such rules — a plumber, arriving to do some repairs in one of the flats, discovered an alligator floating peacefully in the bath.

Once the Barbican Centre was open, the residents had not only acquired a library, but a comfortable cinema as well as the Concert Hall, Theatre and Art Gallery. A large Safeways supermarket opened in Whitecross Street to join the flourishing street-market there, and shopping became less of a problem. "House Groups" were formed and gradually people began to vote for their chosen Common Councilmen in their respective Wards.

It was not perfect. There were occasional wrangles and recriminations; lifts, the residents said, broke down too often; service charges, they claimed, were too high; the waste-disposal system was a failure. The Corporation, gazing in bewilderment at its unruly child, was accused, sometimes unfairly, of not caring. Nevertheless, it was beginning to weld together and to become, for many, their permanent home. The bells of St. Giles' church rang out on Sundays; on week-days flocks of girls chattered their way to school along the Highwalk; the sound of students practising floated across the Estate and ever-increasing audiences, complaining tetchily about the difficulty of finding it, made their way to the Barbican Centre — and enjoyed themselves enormously.

As they had in the past, thousands of City workers poured into the area every week. Among them now came small groups of people who, later in the day, could be spotted standing about in various corners making notes, taking photographs and gazing thoughtfully around them. They were part of a continuous stream of students and town planners who were coming from all over the world to investigate, analyse and write reports on this interesting new exercise in urban redevelopment — the Barbican.

EPILOGUE

*t*oday the Barbican Estate has just celebrated its coming-of-age and the Barbican Centre is approaching its tenth anniversary.

There have been some important changes. In 1981 flats were made available for sale, either on the open market or to tenants at a discount; in January 1990 the Barbican Estate Office reported that 1,280 flats had been sold.

Other buildings have gone up in the surrounding areas and some residents now look out of their windows at very different views. There are new office blocks in Aldersgate Street, an ambitious development in Little Britain is rising fast and a massive building, spanning London Wall, overshadows St. Giles' church. In Golden Lane the Cripplegate Institute has been demolished. A gleaming Health and Fitness Centre flexes its muscles on the corner of Beech Street.

Inside the Estate the trees have grown above the level of the Highwalk — no longer overwhelmed by their environment. More flower-beds, tubs and some inspired landscaping on the North Podium have all contributed to the "greening" of the Barbican and a dolphin fountain, by John Ravera, splashes below Ben Jonson House. The City of London School for Girls has a new annexe (which provoked some lively controversy among the residents before it was built), but the latest addition to the Estate is Charlotte Mayer's sculpture called "Ascent". Standing near concrete air vents on the podium, the graceful spiral, made of stainless steel, does indeed give the impression that it might, at any moment, take off and rise swiftly into the sky.

Barbican Estate: John Ravera's Dolphin Fountain.

And the people who live in the Barbican, the reason after all, for its very existence? There are no simple, clear-cut answers. They are, in general, fairly well off, although there are exceptions even to this rule. Many flats have been sold or rented to companies, providing a short-term and often cosmopolitan population. Others are occupied by people who have retired, by single people who work in or near the City, by students, young couples — and by families. There are, perhaps surprisingly, at least 151 children under five years old living on the Barbican Estate. The Barbican Playgroup (and the Mothers and Toddlers), started fourteen years ago, and run by the mothers themselves, is in great demand and has a long waiting-list. Today the Fann Street Lawn Crèche has also opened off Bridgewater Square.

Some residents have lived here happily since 1969, others have only just arrived. On the whole, little is known about the life-style, habits, hopes and fears of the four thousand or so people living in the Barbican. They probably prefer it that way.

It has been a long, exciting, and sometimes turbulent twenty-one years. At last there is time to sit back, assess the present, plan for the future and, above all perhaps, time to appreciate an astonishing achievement. The Barbican, for all its problems in the past, exists as a large and vital community — a community built on destruction and sitting proudly on its history.

This could not have been accomplished without the courageous vision of members of the Corporation of the City of London — or

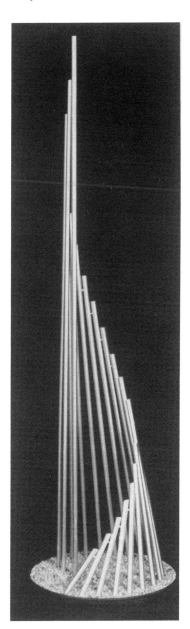

Maquette for Charlotte Mayer's sculpture 'Ascent'.

without the inspired daring of the architects, who picked up the challenge and turned a vision into reality.

ANDREWES HOUSE: Lancelot Andrewes (1555-1626) — theologian, famous preacher, Vicar of St. Giles for seventeen years. Eventually Bishop of Winchester.

BRANDON MEWS: Robert Brandon (14th Century) — Earl of Suffolk. Granted the Manor of Basecourt (known as Barbican), by Edward III in 1336.

BRETON HOUSE: Nicholas Breton (1553-1625) — poet, satirist. Lived in Barbican area.

BRYER COURT: W. Bryer and Sons (19th-20th Centuries), gold and silver refiners, watchmakers etc. Premises in Barbican Street.

BUNYAN COURT: John Bunyan (1628-1688), preacher, author of *The Pilgrim's Progress*. Preached in Monkwell Street, buried in Bunhill Fields.

CROMWELL TOWER: Oliver Cromwell (1599-1658), soldier, statesman, Lord Protector of the Commonwealth. Married Elizabeth Bourchier at St. Giles' Church.

DEFOE HOUSE: Daniel Defoe (1660-1731), journalist, author of *Robinson Crusoe* etc. Probably born in Fore Street. Died in Ropemaker Street and buried in Bunhill Fields.

FROBISHER CRESCENT: Sir Martin Frobisher (1535-1594), sailor. Knighted during the 'Battle of the Armada'. Buried St. Giles' Cripplegate.

GILBERT HOUSE: Sir Humphrey Gilbert (1539-1583) explorer, soldier, sailor. Drowned off the Azores following successful expedition to Newfoundland: lived at one time in Redcross Street.

LAMBERT JONES MEWS: Richard Lambert Jones (b. 1783). Member of the Court of

Common Council for the ward of Cripplegate Without. Chairman of Library Committee for nineteen years.

BEN JONSON HOUSE: Ben Jonson (1572-1637), actor, playwright, (*Bartholomew Fair* etc). Lived for some years in the parish of Cripplegate.

LAUDERDALE TOWER: John Maitland created first Earl of Lauderdale by Charles I in 1624. One of his homes was Lauderdale House on Aldersgate Street.

MILTON COURT: John Milton (1608-1674). Poet, author of *Paradise Lost* (1667) and *Paradise Regained* (1671). Lived for some time in Barbican area. Buried St. Giles Cripplegate.

THOMAS MORE HOUSE: Sir Thomas More (1478-1535), statesman, author, lawyer: imprisoned in the Tower of London and eventually beheaded. Born in Cripplegate Parish.

MOUNTJOY HOUSE: Christopher Mountjoy, Huguenot refugee who came to London in 1572. Made women's headdresses and lived in Silver Street.

SEDDON HOUSE: George Seddon (d1801), Master cabinet maker. Established huge furniture emporium in Aldersgate Street.

SHAKESPEARE TOWER: William Shakespeare (1564-1616). Actor, poet, playwright. Born in Stratford-Upon-Avon but spent most of his working life in London. Known to have lodged at the Mountjoys' in Silver Street in 1604.

SPEED HOUSE: John Speed (1552-1629), Merchant Tailor, historian and cartographer. Produced a series of maps of the counties of England and Wales. Buried St. Giles Cripplegate.

JOHN TRUNDLE COURT: John Trundle (c. 1600), stationer. Premises in the Barbican. Published, with Nicholas Ling, the first quarto of William Shakespeare's *Hamlet*.

WILLOUGHBY HOUSE: Catharine Willoughby, Duchess of Suffolk (1520-1580). Upholder of the new 'Protestant' beliefs. Taunted Bishop Gardiner and later forced to flee abroad temporarily from her home in the Barbican.